WELCOME TO THE WORLD OF
Spirit Bears

Diane Swanson

WALRUS
B O O K S

To Bonnie Chapman, teacher-librarian at Hillcrest Elementary School in Surrey,
British Columbia, who suggested the topic for this book

Copyright © 2007 by Diane Swanson
Whitecap Books

Edited by Nadine Boyd
Proofread by Ben D'Andrea
Cover design by Steve Penner and Jesse Marchand
Interior design by Margaret Ng
Typeset by Jesse Marchand
Photo research by Nadine Boyd
Cover photograph by Simon Jackson
Photo credits: Robert Franz 14; Peter Zweirs 12, 16, 18;
    Marni Grossman 6, 22, 24; Simon Jackson iv, 2, 4, 8, 10, 12, 26

Printed and bound in China by WKT

For more information
on this series and other
Whitecap Books titles,
visit our website at
www.whitecap.ca.

Library and Archives Canada Cataloguing in Publication

Swanson, Diane, 1944-
    Welcome to the world of spirit bears / Diane Swanson.
ISBN-13: 978-1-55285-847-9
ISBN-10: 1-55285-847-2
    1. Kermode bear--Juvenile literature. I. Title.
QL737.C27A93 2007   j599.78'5   C2006-904979-3

The publisher acknowledges the financial support of the Canada Council for the Arts, the British Columbia Arts Council, and the Government of Canada through the Book Publishing Industry Development Program (BPIDP). Whitecap Books also acknowledges the financial support of the Province of British Columbia through the Book Publishing Tax Credit.

Contents

World of Difference

ENTER THE WORLD OF SPIRIT BEARS. They're black bears that are white — or that are black but are able to have white cubs. Black bears normally vary in color from brown to cinnamon to gray-blue to black. Only very few have white fur. In fact, in the spirit bears' main home of Princess Royal Island in the province of British Columbia, just one in ten is white.

Spirit bears have other names too. They're called kermode [ker-MOH-dee] bears — after Francis Kermode, who studied them in the early 1900s. Sometimes they're labeled ghost bears because they can be difficult to find.

The majestic white spirit bear fascinates people.

1

A black spirit bear blends well with a dark rock wall.

Never mistake a white spirit bear for an albino [al-BYE-no] bear or a polar bear. The albino bear is a rare quirk of nature. It has white fur, but unlike the spirit bear, it has no color in its skin or eyes. Although the polar bear has white fur, it lives farther north and is a lot larger than the spirit bear.

Still, the spirit bear is a good size. An average male weighs as much as the washer and dryer that launder your clothes. The male is about twice as heavy as the female.

The spirit bear shares many features with other black bears. It has rounded ears, small eyes, long nostrils, and a short tail. Each of its feet has five sharp, curved claws.

When the spirit bear moves, it often just shuffles its bulky body. But don't be fooled. If it must, this bear can run faster than a car usually drives through town.

SPIRIT BEAR LEGEND

The First Nations, or native people, of Canada's Pacific coast tell an ancient story of a time when snow and ice buried Earth. Raven, their creator of the world, chose to make the land lush and green.

But Raven wanted people to remember when Earth was white with snow. So he flew among the black bears and turned every tenth one white. Raven also kept a rainforest home for the ghostly spirit bears so they could live in peace.

Where in the World

THE SPIRIT BEAR IS SPECIAL — so special that in 2006, British Columbians made it an emblem of their province. They also set aside land for the bear by preserving rainforests on the Pacific coast, especially on Princess Royal Island.

Like all black bears, spirit bears prefer land covered with thick woods and bush. Rainforests give them food and shelter. Set far away from cities, these forests are places where the bears can roam freely — even during daylight.

When autumn comes to the Pacific coast, spirit bears hunt for dens — cozy nooks

In a damp Pacific rainforest, the spirit bear finds a good home.

A dimly lit den makes a cozy bed for a spirit bear's winter rest.

where they can sleep through cold winters. The dens they choose might be caves, hollow logs, rotten tree trunks, or openings in rock piles. These dens are usually just big enough for the bears to curl up inside. Sometimes the bears scrape the walls of their dens to make them bigger.

Male bears often wait for snow to fall before denning down. Females move into their dens sooner, lining them with soft grass, wood chips, or leaves.

Drawing on the fat that's stored in their bodies, the bears can sleep for months without eating anything. Their hearts beat more slowly during their winter sleep, but like other bears, spirit bears waken easily if disturbed. If they're startled by a loud noise, for example, the bears may head out to look for new dens.

SIMON'S SPIRIT

When Simon Jackson of British Columbia was only 13 years old, he began a campaign to promote the spirit bear. His message? Tell everyone that the white black bear is real and that it needs a safe home.

Through meetings, speeches, and letters, Simon encouraged thousands of people — including Prince William of the United Kingdom — to speak up for the bear. He also formed the Spirit Bear Youth Coalition, which works to save the rainforests that the spirit bear needs.

World Full of Food

SUPERSIZED SERVINGS OF ALMOST EVERYTHING. That's what spirit bears eat — spring, summer, and autumn. They graze on grass and nibble on shrubs. They gobble berries, crunch nuts, and munch insects. They also fish for salmon and hunt animals such as mice. The bears are heavy drinkers and gulp water throughout the day.

Spirit bears have no trouble getting food. With their powerful paws, they dig for roots, rip into rotting logs, and overturn rocks. Their front feet are nimble enough to strip leaves from branches and to snatch slender snakes as they sleep in the sun. Limber lips

Spirit bears eat almost anything they can find.

9

Got it! A spirit bear catches a fish for dinner.

and long tongues help guide small food into the bears' mouths.

When spirit bears fish, some stand firmly on shore and reach out for the swimming salmon. Others wade in rivers to seize the fish. At times, the bears dive right into the water. They can even swim beneath sunken logs to grab slippery salmon.

Compared with dark-colored bears, white spirit bears usually spend more hours eating and drinking during the heat of summer. White fur tends to help the bears stay cooler.

By late autumn, the spirit bears are fat. They stop feeding before entering their dens for a long sleep. Over winter, they might lose nearly a third of their body weight. Then they're eager to stuff themselves with food again.

BEAR-SALMON-TREE CYCLE

Like other bears on British Columbia's coast, the spirit bears often drag salmon into forests to feed. But the bears may leave as much as half the salmon lying on the forest floor. The rotting fish fertilize the soil, which helps the trees grow.

In return, the trees' roots prevent heavy rains from washing the soil into streams. That keeps clear and clean the water where the salmon lay their eggs. And more eggs mean more salmon for the bears to eat.

World of Words

SPIRIT BEAR TALK ISN'T ALL HUFFING AND PUFFING. The bears also speak through body language, odors, and scratches.

For example, a bear may slap the ground to say that it's fearful, then sit still, look away, and yawn to announce it wants to be left alone. When one bear moves close to another and opens its jaws wide, it's likely saying, "Hey! Notice me."

At breeding times, the male spirit bear spreads his urine around to attract females and warn competing males to stay away. The smell of his urine tells other bears his sex and age. It also says that he's interested

A spirit bear attracts attention by spreading its strong jaws.

13

in finding a mate.

Spirit bears often treat trees as message boards. They stand on their hind legs and rub the tree trunks with their heads and backs. What's more, they may bite or claw the trunks. The odors and scratches they leave help them claim the surrounding areas as their own. Male bears even use these tree trunk message boards to advertise for mates.

Standing tall, a spirit bear rubs a tree to leave a message.

Many of the sounds that spirit bears make are quiet. Just by clicking their tongues or grunting faintly, females can call to their cubs. The bears may voice pain by bawling softly and express fear by moaning. They sometimes threaten other bears by making low, throbbing noises. But loud sounds — clacking teeth or heavy blowing — can mean they're afraid or have been scared by something, such as having a bad fall.

BLUFFING BEARS

Like many other animals, spirit bears often bluff to avoid fights. After all, fighting uses up a lot of energy. It can also injure the bears.

When something or someone threatens a spirit bear, the bear flattens its ears, crouches close to the ground, and rushes toward the threat. Then it stops short at the very last second. Sometimes the bear makes loud noises as it charges. The point of this bluff is to scare the enemy. It means "Go away."

New World

IT'S A WINTRY WORLD WHEN CUBS ARE BORN. Spirit bear mothers are tucked inside their dens, usually fast asleep. While they're resting, they give birth — often to two or more cubs.

When the bear cubs first arrive, they're fragile. Each one weighs only as much as a pear, and they're seldom longer than a soup spoon. What's more, the newborns don't have any teeth yet, and their eyes are tightly closed.

The tiny bear cubs nestle against their mother. Heat from her body and her thick fur help keep them warm. They feed by sucking

Just out of its den, a spirit bear cub peeks at its world.

Two spirit bear cubs
prepare to take on life.

the rich milk she produces.

Newborn cubs can fill a den with a soft, pulsing noise like the purring of kittens. It's a sound they make whenever they're content — even as they grow. Adult bears "purr" when they feel very comfortable or well fed, although their sound is deeper than the one that cubs make.

If a mother bear wakens during winter, she nuzzles one of her cubs dozily. Sometimes she licks its head before falling back to sleep. But the cubs develop quickly on their own. As they get bigger, they open their eyes and grow teeth. By spring, they're ready to leave the den. Still, the cubs depend on their mother to keep them safe and teach them how to survive in the outside world.

COLOR OF CUBS

Black or white? The color of spirit bears is decided before they're born. It depends on their genes, which are the basic units of heredity. Like all animals, spirit bear cubs get their genes from their parents.

To have white fur, spirit bear cubs must inherit white fur genes from both parents — even if the parents themselves are black. Interestingly, the bears pay no attention to the color differences among them.

Small World

SPIRIT BEAR CUBS HAVE LOTS TO LEARN. They spend months following their mother and trying to do what she does. Many of their lessons focus on food. Although the young bears feed on their mother's milk until late summer, they also chew solids. The cubs learn where to graze grass and how to pick berries from a bush. They may watch their mother take honey from a beehive or nab a fat frog from a stream. Some mother bears teach the tricks of getting food by flinging a fish to shore, then letting the cubs kill and eat it.

The cubs learn to use their super senses

Spirit bear cubs learn to climb a tree where they'll be safe.

of smell and hearing. Their noses can detect the distant stench of rotting meat. Their ears can catch the sound of mice scurrying through fallen leaves.

Keen senses also warn the cubs of enemies such as eagles, wolves, and adult male bears. Big male bears are the cubs' greatest threat. But while the young bears are learning to escape danger, their mother will fight to

A mother spirit bear shows her cub how to catch fish.

the death to protect them.

By the following winter, the spirit bear cubs may be able to fend for themselves. However, they usually enter a den with their mother, then leave the family when spring arrives.

The number of lines that run across the bears' teeth reveals their age — one line for every year lived. If the bears have led safe, food-filled lives, their teeth may have more than 20 lines.

SAFETY IN TREES

To spirit bears, a tree offers more than shelter. It provides safety, too. When a mother bear leads her cubs from their winter den, she sometimes makes a nest beneath a big tree. Then she can keep a close eye on the cubs.

If danger threatens, the mother bear signals her cubs with a HUFF! They climb the tree — fast — while she stands guard. The cubs stay in the tree until they hear their mother grunt. Then they know it's safe to climb down.

Fun World

ALL BEARS PLAY GAMES — and spirit bears are no exception. Active play helps adult bears stay fit. And it helps cubs exercise their growing muscles and bones. Through play, the cubs practice hunting and fishing — skills they'll need when they're living on their own.

The bears invite partners to play games by slapping them gently. Cubs usually romp with other cubs but sometimes play with their mothers.

One bear may stalk another in play. The stalker creeps slowly through the woods, moving behind bushes and trees to hide

It's time for play! Two spirit bear cubs romp around.

An adult spirit bear sometimes splashes in water just for fun.

along the way. Suddenly, it pounces on the second bear and lightly bites its ears.

A heavy pounce can lead to a wrestling match between the two bears. They tumble over and over, shaking their heads from side to side. But they're careful to angle their claws so that they don't cause any injuries.

Spirit bears like to chase each other, too. One bear may scoot up a tree to "escape," or it may turn and start a play-fight. The bears "fight" with their jaws wide open and almost touching.

Sometimes, spirit bears play by themselves. They might splash around in the water or "fish" by springing on sticks that float in streams. The bears might even fling the sticks ashore as if they were real fish.

SPIRIT BEAR SURPRISES

Spirit bears amaze people. Here are some reasons why:

🐾 Spirits bears are good swimmers. They can easily cross rivers — even underwater.

🐾 As bulky as they are, spirit bears can use a back foot to scratch an itchy ear.

🐾 Climbing is easy for spirit bears. They grab tree trunks with their front paws and push up with their back paws.

🐾 Spirit bears can drop to the forest floor from tree branches higher than the roofs of some houses.

Index